Quiz Champs

Life Cycles

Manisha Nayak

WS Education

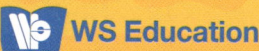

NEW JERSEY • LONDON • SINGAPORE • BEIJING • SHANGHAI • HONG KONG • TAIPEI • CHENNAI • TOKYO

Published by

WS Education, an imprint of
World Scientific Publishing Co. Pte. Ltd.
5 Toh Tuck Link, Singapore 596224
USA office: 27 Warren Street, Suite 401-402, Hackensack, NJ 07601
UK office: 57 Shelton Street, Covent Garden, London WC2H 9HE

National Library Board, Singapore Cataloguing in Publication Data
Name(s): Nayak, Manisha.
Title: Life cycles / Manisha Nayak.
Other Title(s): Quiz champs.
Description: Singapore : WS Education, [2024]
Identifier(s): ISBN 978-981-12-7463-3 (hardback) | 978-981-12-7492-3 (paperback) |
    978-981-12-7464-0 (ebook for institutions) | 978-981-12-7465-7 (ebook for individuals)
Subject(s): LCSH: Life cycles (Biology)--Juvenile literature.
Classification: DDC 571.8--dc23

British Library Cataloguing-in-Publication Data
A catalogue record for this book is available from the British Library.

All photos from Shutterstock.com.

Copyright © 2024 by World Scientific Publishing Co. Pte. Ltd.

All rights reserved. This book, or parts thereof, may not be reproduced in any form or by any means, electronic or mechanical, including photocopying, recording or any information storage and retrieval system now known or to be invented, without written permission from the publisher.

For photocopying of material in this volume, please pay a copying fee through the Copyright Clearance Center, Inc., 222 Rosewood Drive, Danvers, MA 01923, USA. In this case permission to photocopy is not required from the publisher.

Design and layout by Rosie Gowsell Pattison/Plan B Book Packagers

Desk editor: Daniele Lee

Printed in Singapore

Welcome to the wonderful World of Science!

How to use this book

- Read the questions on the following pages and try to guess the correct answers.

- You can start at the beginning of the book or do the quizzes in any order.

- Do the quizzes by yourself or with a friend or family member.

- Keep score to see how many answers you get right.

- At the end of the book, you'll find a bonus quiz where you can match keywords to their meanings.

- You'll also find a bonus crossword puzzle, which you can use to decipher a password to unlock a special *Quiz Champs* certificate!

> Find me, your Quiz Champs host, hidden in 25 pictures in this book. (Answers on page 167.)

> Hi! I'm Carter, part-time caterpillar and part-time quizmaster!

In this edition of *Quiz Champs*, you'll test your knowledge and learn more about the fascinating life cycles of plants and animals!

You'll also find:

Jokes and riddles to make you giggle

Heehee!

Did You Know?
Boxes filled with fun and unusual facts about life cycles

Cycles are changes that repeat themselves. Day and night make up a cycle. Day comes after night and night comes after day in a cycle.

Cycles occur in living things too. These are known as life cycles. For example, humans change as they grow over time. Babies become children, teenagers and then adults. Adults are able to reproduce and have babies. Thus, the life cycle continues.

Different living things have different stages in their life cycles.

Ready to see how much you know about life cycles? Turn the page and let's go!

What are the three stages in the life cycle of a flowering plant?

A root, stem and leaf
B flower, fruit and seed
C fruit, young plant and tree
D seed, young plant and adult plant

Turn the page for the answer!

7

ANSWER:

Flowering plants have three stages in their life cycle—the seed, the young plant and the adult plant. Not all plants are flowering plants. The life cycle of non-flowering plants is different from the life cycle of flowering plants.

seed

young plant

Did You Know?
Flowering plants only bear flowers and fruits in the adult stage.

adult plant

What did the young corn plant call its dad?

Pop-corn!

TRUE or FALSE?

A tomato is a fruit.

Turn the page for the answer!

11

ANSWER: **True!**

The part of a flowering plant that contains seeds is known as the fruit. Scientifically, tomatoes are actually fruits, though we call them 'vegetables' in everyday language.

Did You Know?

Many of the vegetables you eat are actually fruits in the scientific sense. Some examples are eggplant, lady's finger, capsicum and pumpkin.

Why did the tomato plant in the garden grow so quickly?

It was trying to ketchup to the other plants!

At which stage of its life cycle does an apple tree have flowers?

- Ⓐ the seed stage
- Ⓑ the young plant stage
- Ⓒ the adult stage
- Ⓓ all of the above

Turn the page for the answer!

ANSWER: **C** — **the adult stage**

Flowers are not just pretty to look at. They play an important part in helping plants to reproduce. When an apple tree reaches the adult stage, it produces flowers. The flowers develop into fruits that contain seeds. The seeds grow into new plants.

Did You Know?

Apples float on water! This is due to the fact that they contain a lot of air.

What is the process of a seed growing into a young plant called?

ANSWER: Germination.

A seed will germinate, or start to sprout, into a young plant if it gets enough air, water and warmth. Not all seeds grow into new plants though! Seeds only germinate under the right conditions.

Did You Know?

Some seeds can stay dormant (in a resting state) for years before they get the right conditions to grow into new plants!

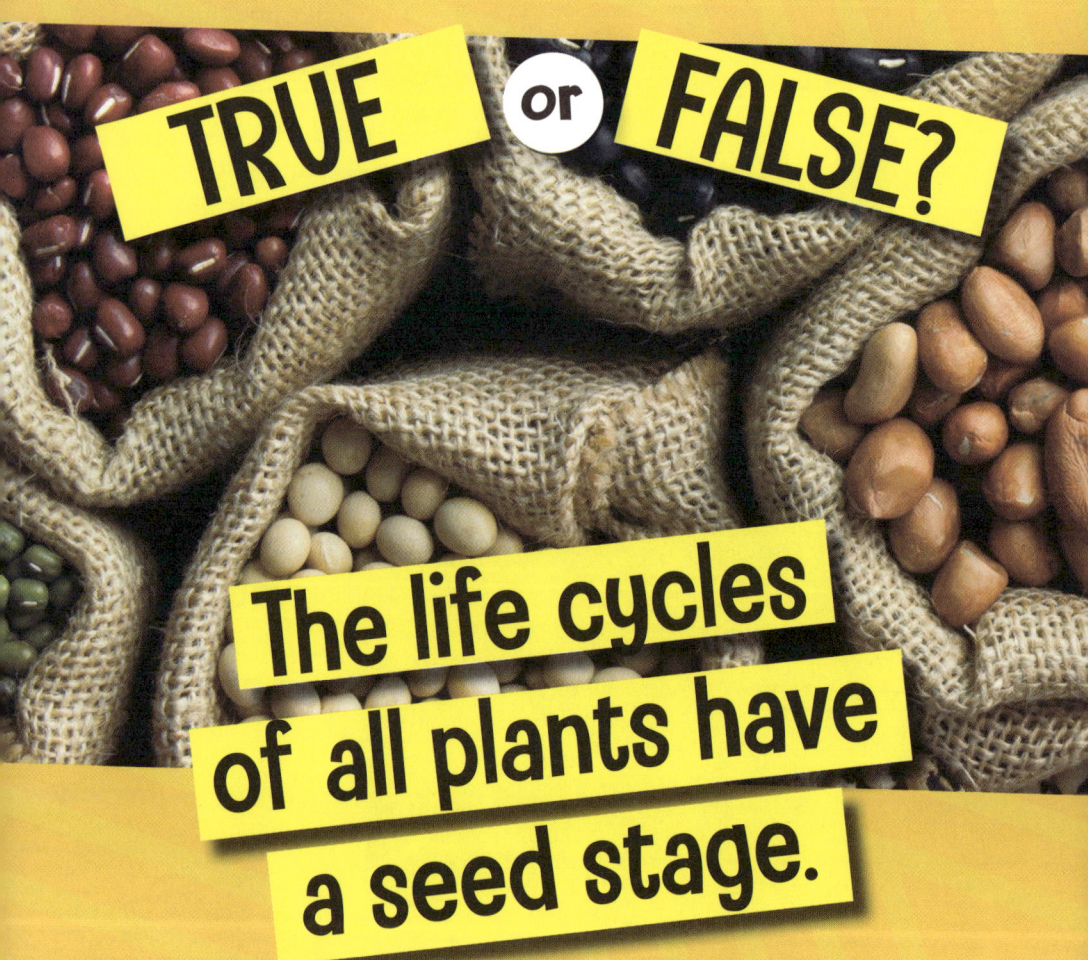

TRUE or FALSE?

The life cycles of all plants have a seed stage.

20

ANSWER: False!

Not all plants reproduce from seeds. Some plants, such as ferns, reproduce from spores. Plants that reproduce from spores have different life cycle stages as compared to plants that reproduce from seeds.

What kind of car does a fern drive?

A spores car!

Which fruit has the world's largest seed?

coconut

avocado

cacao pod

- **A** a coconut
- **B** an avocado
- **C** a cacao pod
- **D** a coco de mer

Turn the page for the answer!

coco de mer

ANSWER: **D**

a coco de mer

The coco de mer is a palm tree found in the Seychelles islands, in the Indian Ocean. It has the largest seed in the world, weighing up to 18 kilograms! That's as heavy as an average five-year-old child!

TRUE or FALSE? All animals reproduce by laying eggs.

26

ANSWER: False!

All birds, and most fish, insects and reptiles, lay eggs. However, most mammals reproduce by giving birth. There are only two mammals that lay eggs—the platypus and the echidna.

How did the turtle feel after laying her eggs?

Eggs-hausted!

Which of these animals does NOT reproduce by laying eggs?

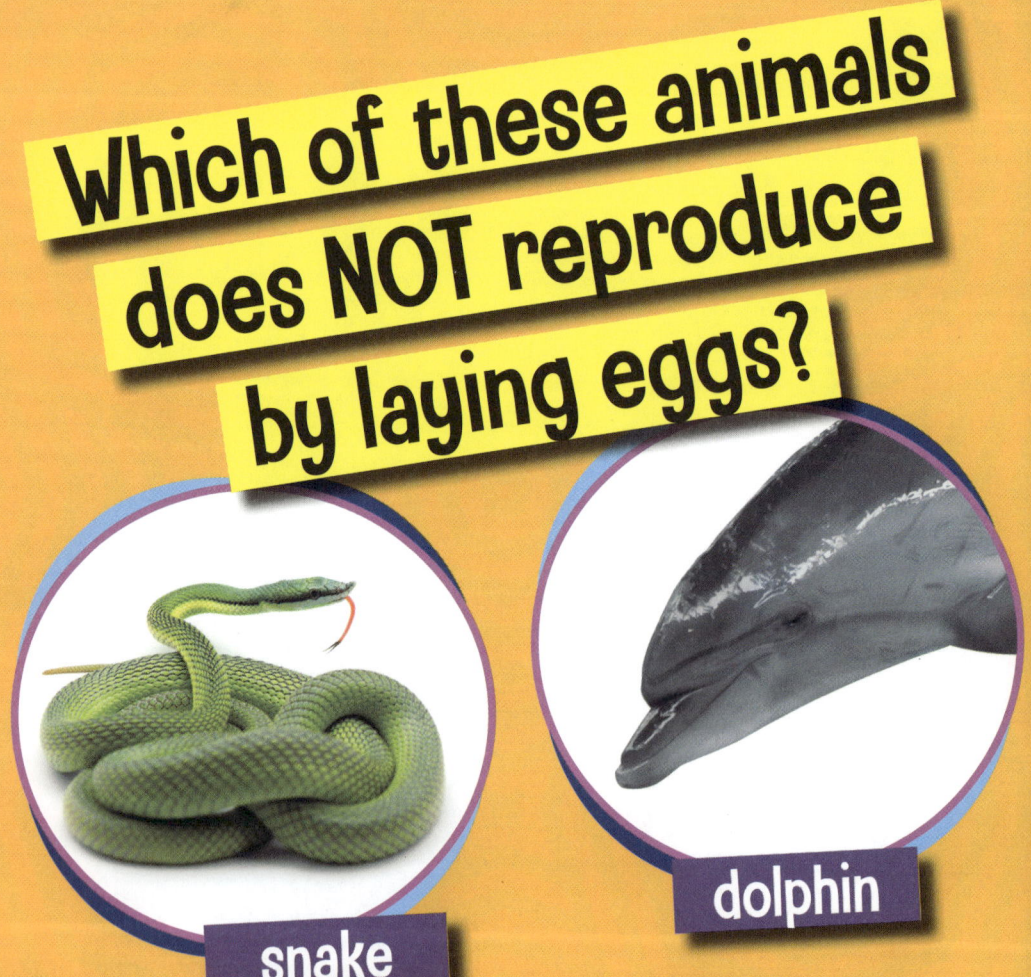

snake

dolphin

ANSWER: **B**

a dolphin

A dolphin is a mammal. Most mammals reproduce by giving birth. They feed their young with mother's milk.

Did You Know?

Newborn dolphins drink their mother's milk every 20 minutes, 24 hours a day!

Which animal lays the world's largest eggs?

ostrich

penguin

32

blue whale

crocodile

- **A** an ostrich
- **B** a penguin
- **C** a crocodile
- **D** a blue whale

Turn the page for the answer!

33

ANSWER:

an ostrich

The egg of an ostrich weighs about 1.5 kilograms. That's about the same as 24 chicken eggs!

Did You Know?

Ostriches share nests. Several females lay their eggs in a common nest that can hold about 60 eggs!

Which bird is the wealthiest?

The ost-*rich*!

35

Why does the parent bird bring food to the chick?

ANSWER:
The chick is not yet able to fly to find its own food. When the chicks hatch out of the eggs, they are not strong enough to fly. Till they grow stronger and their wings develop fully, their parents need to bring food to them.

Which bird lays its eggs in the nests of other birds?

crow

mynah

kingfisher

cuckoo

- **A** the crow
- **B** the mynah
- **C** the cuckoo
- **D** the kingfisher

Turn the page for the answer!

39

cuckoo chick

ANSWER: C

the cuckoo

The female cuckoo bird visits other birds' nests and lays her eggs in them. Sometimes, she will pick a nest where the other eggs look like her own. This helps to deceive the nest's owners, who take care of the cuckoo's eggs like their own. When the cuckoo chick hatches, it may even push the other eggs or chicks out of the nest! The nest's owners will continue to feed and raise the cuckoo chick.

What animal is hatching from this egg?

ANSWER: A crocodile.

Crocodiles are reptiles. Most reptiles reproduce by laying eggs. A baby crocodile looks very similar to an adult crocodile. Some adult crocodiles are 10,000 times heavier than baby crocodiles!

What is wrong with this picture?

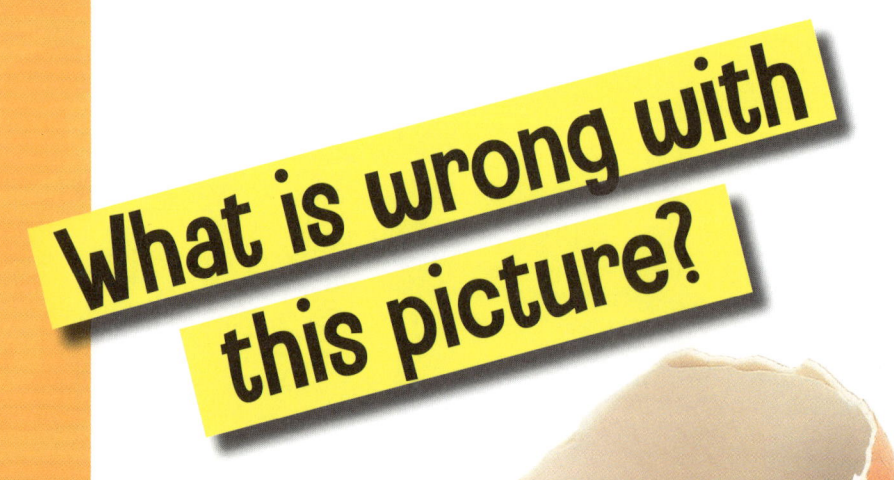

44

What did the mama elephant say to the naughty baby elephant?

T(u)sk t(u)sk!

ANSWER: Elephants don't hatch from eggs! An elephant is a mammal. Most mammals reproduce by giving birth to live young.

45

TRUE or FALSE?

What is black, white and blue?

A *sad* panda!

46

A newborn panda is 900 times smaller than its mother.

ANSWER: True!

A newborn panda is lighter than a banana, weighing only about 100 grams at birth. The panda's mother, on the other hand, can weigh about 90 kilograms!

47

What is the young of a kangaroo called?

48

ANSWER: A joey.
A kangaroo is a marsupial. Marsupials are animals that are born incompletely developed. The joey is carried and nursed in a pouch on the mother's belly.

What kind of music do kangaroos like?

Hip-hop!

49

What kind of baby bird is this?

50

A. an owl
B. a duck
C. a penguin
D. a flamingo

ANSWER:
D a flamingo

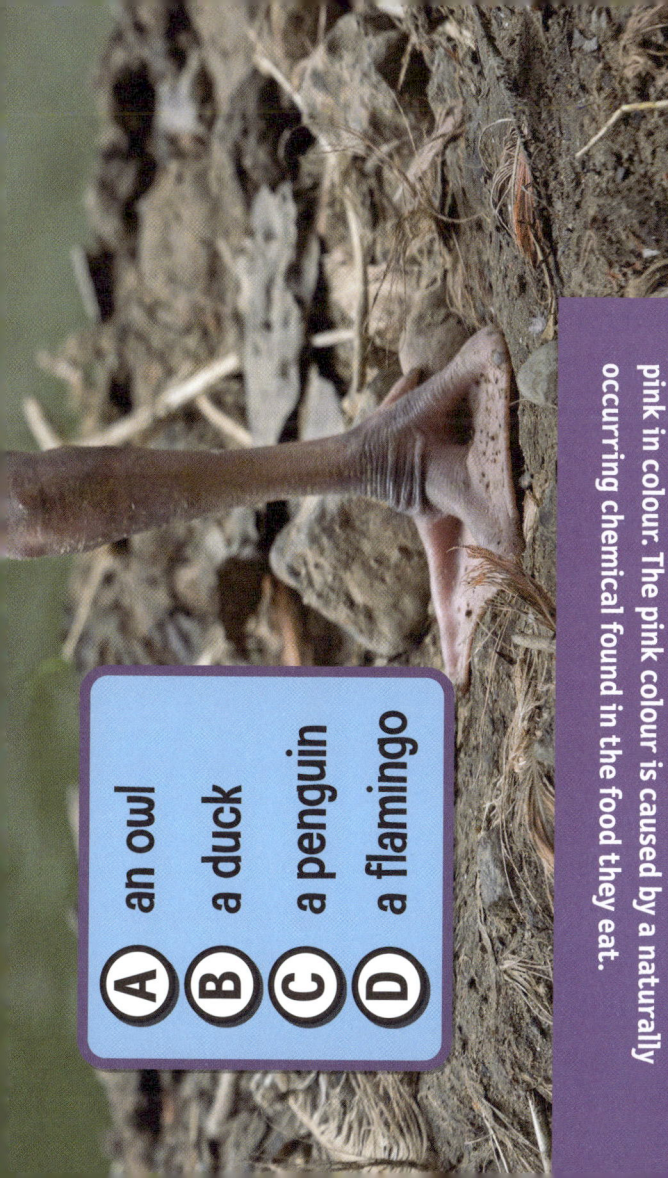

Flamingo chicks are white, while adult flamingos are pink in colour. The pink colour is caused by a naturally occurring chemical found in the food they eat.

What do you get when you set the letter 'O' on fire?

A flaming-o!

51

How long are African elephants pregnant for?

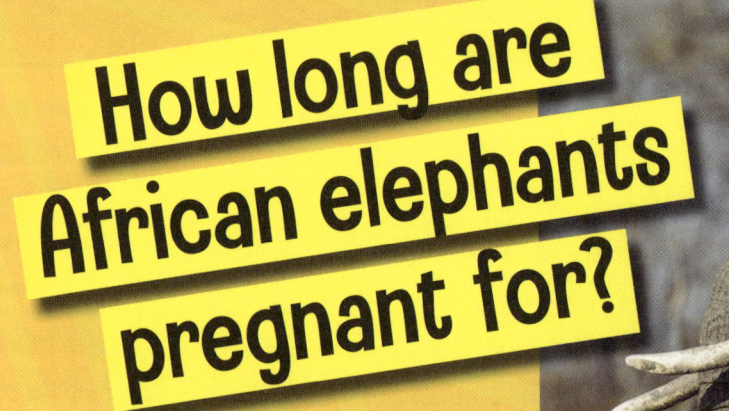

- **A** about 1 month
- **B** about 9 months
- **C** about 1 year
- **D** about 2 years

Turn the page for the answer!

52

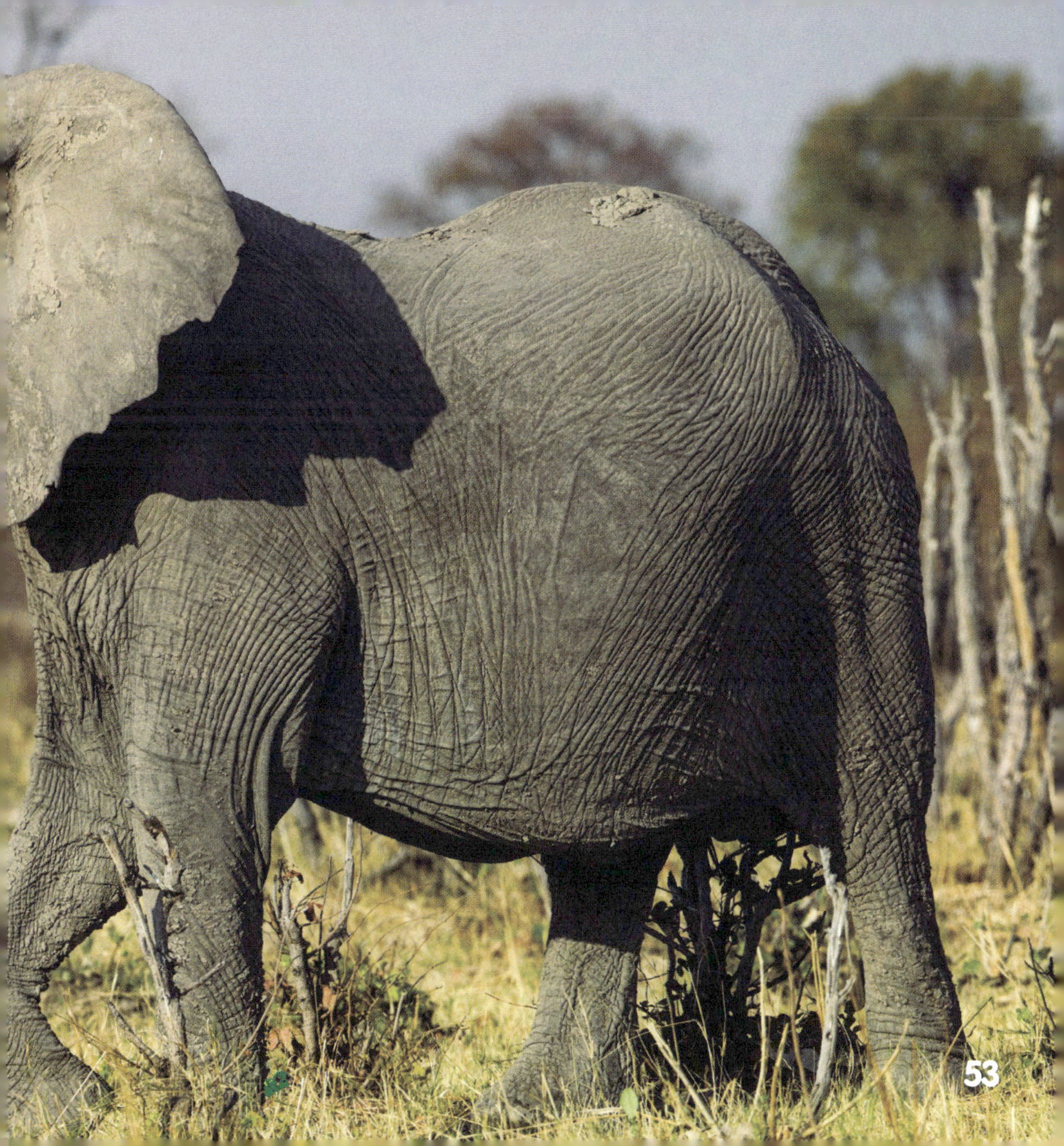

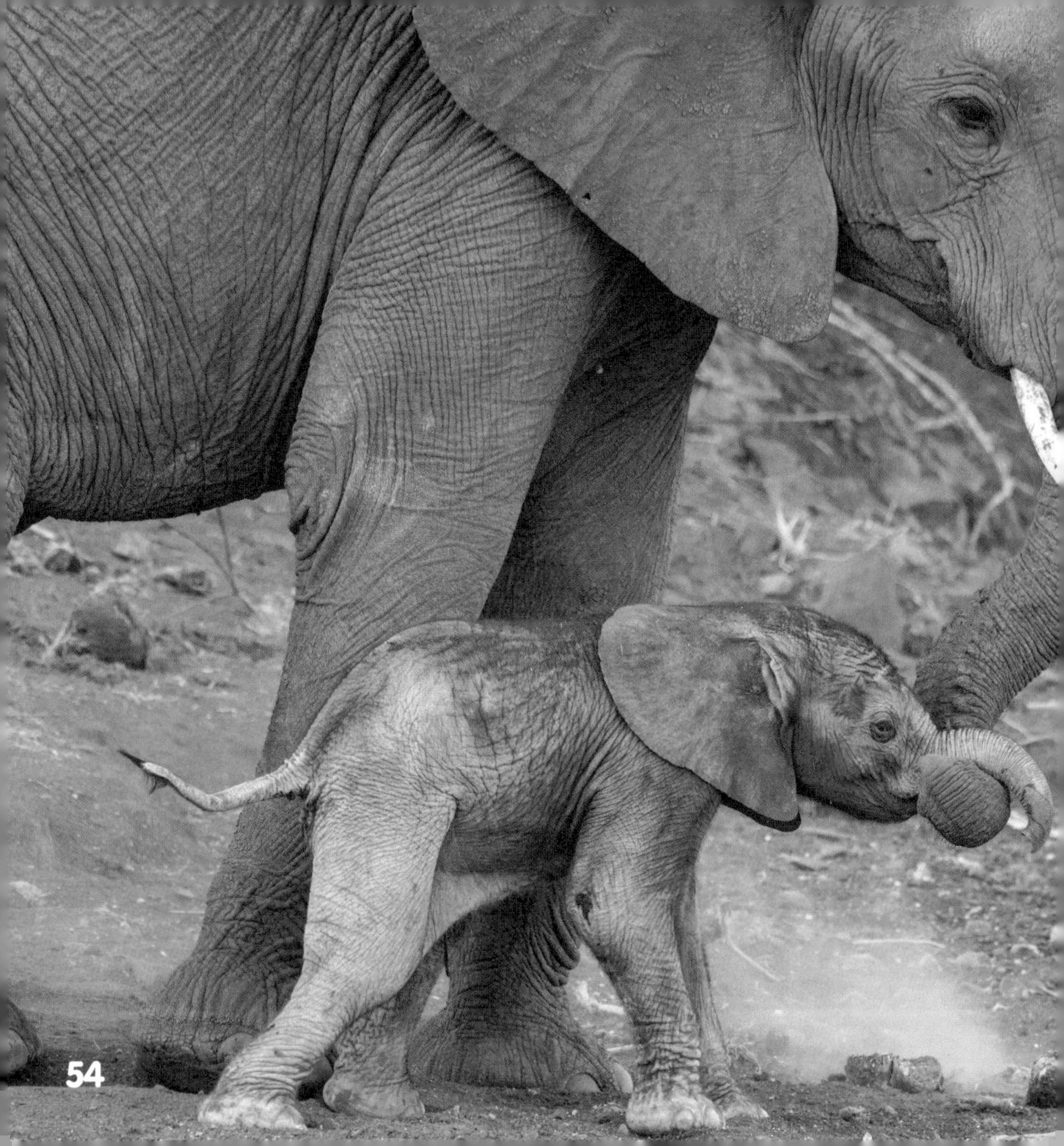

ANSWER: **D**

about 2 years

Elephants are mammals and give birth to their young. African elephants have the longest pregnancies of all land animals. They are pregnant for about 22 months.

Did You Know?

A newborn elephant weighs almost 100 kilograms. That's about as much as 200 soccer balls!

Which of the arrows is wrong in this life cycle of a chicken?

56

A

B

Turn the page for the answer!

57

ANSWER:

Arrow C.

The life cycle of a chicken has three stages — egg, young and adult. Arrow C should point from the adult to the egg.

C

A

B

59

What is an unborn or unhatched animal known as?

How does a chick leave its egg?

Through the eggs-it!

A the ova
B the yolk
C the embryo
D the egg white

Did You Know?
A fertilised hen's egg takes about 21 days to hatch into a chick.

ANSWER: C the embryo
An embryo forms when an egg is fertilised during the mating of a male and a female animal. The eggs that most of us eat are unfertilised. They do not have embryos.

61

What is the purpose of the yolk of an egg?

- **A** to protect the embryo
- **B** to help the egg to hatch
- **C** to develop into the embryo
- **D** to provide food for the embryo

Turn the page for the answer!

ANSWER: D

to provide food for the embryo

The transparent part of the egg is known as the egg white and the yellow part is known as the yolk. The yolk contains most of the nutrients found in the egg.

What do you call a person who knows everything about eggs?

An eggs-pert!

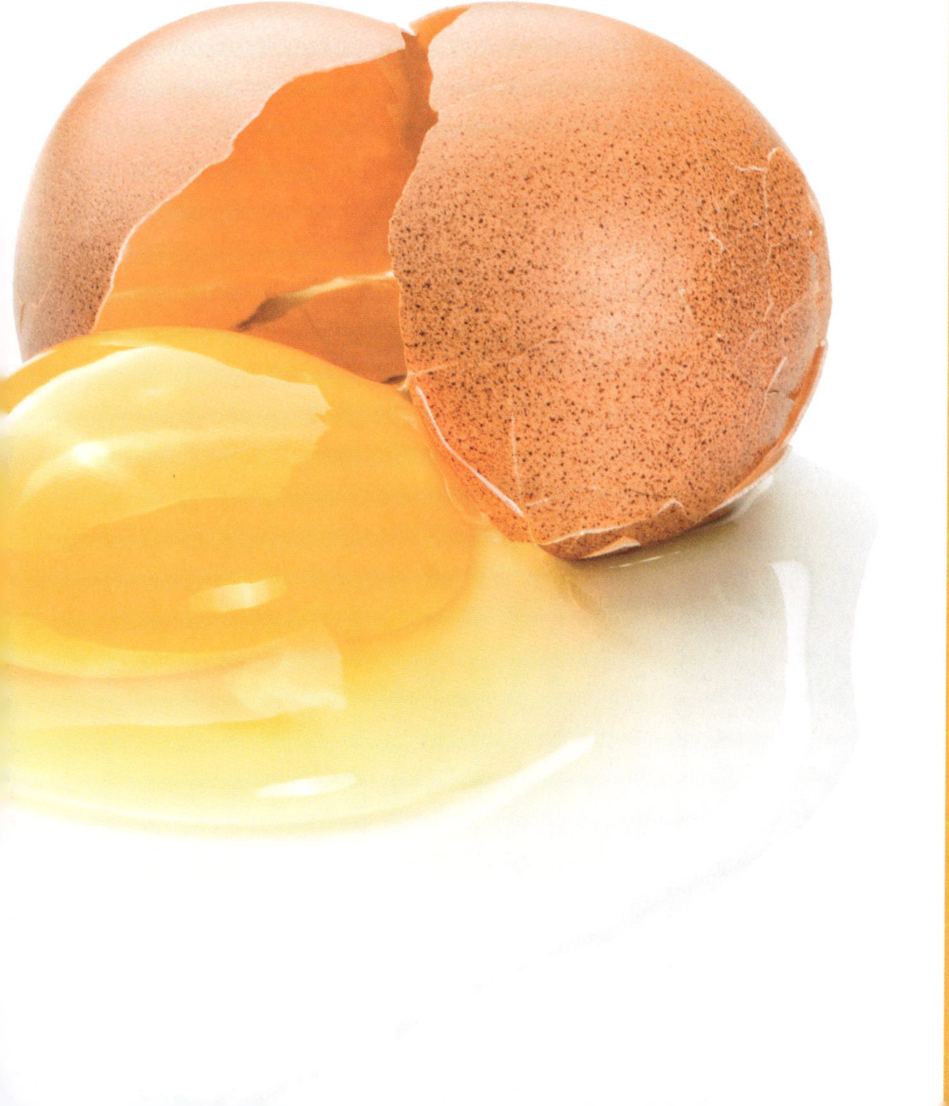

Why does a hen sit on her eggs?

ANSWER: To keep them warm.

A hen sits on her eggs to keep them warm. This helps the embryo in the egg develop till it is ready to hatch. If an egg is not kept warm, the embryo will not develop properly.

Did You Know?

A hen turns her eggs about 50 times a day. This helps maintain an even temperature and prevents the embryo from sticking to the side of the egg.

Which device is used to hatch eggs without a hen on some farms?

- (A) an oximeter
- (B) an incubator
- (C) an excavator
- (D) a thermometer

ANSWER:

B) an incubator

An incubator is a device that can help to hatch eggs by maintaining them under the same conditions that a hen would. Factors such as temperature and humidity (the amount of moisture in the air) are strictly controlled so the eggs can hatch. Some incubators can also turn the eggs regularly, just like a hen does!

Which bird do these eggs belong to?

- **A** the Iceland gull
- **B** the Indian peacock
- **C** the American robin
- **D** the Egyptian goose

ANSWER: c) the American robin

The eggs of the American robin are blue in colour. This is due to the presence of a pigment called biliverdin. Many scientists believe that the blue colour of the egg helps protect the embryo from the sun's harmful rays.

71

What will these young animals grow to become?

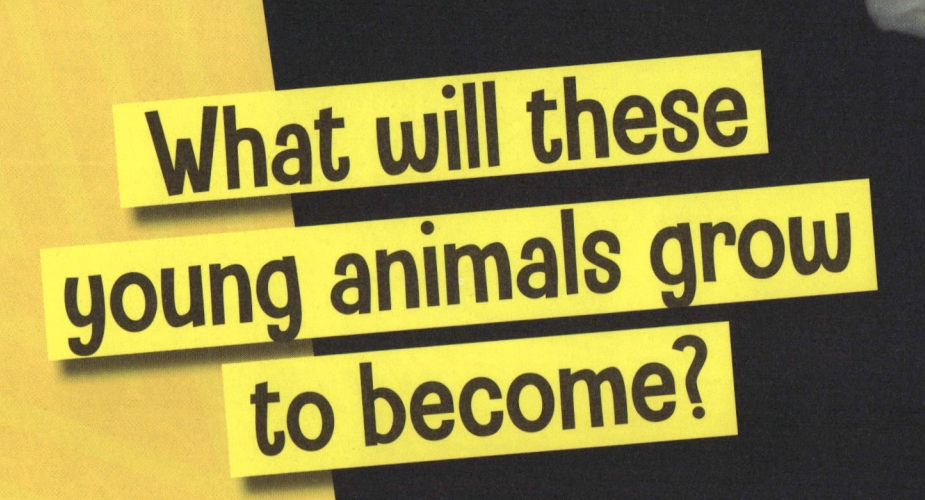

72

- **A** fish
- **B** frogs
- **C** snakes
- **D** worms

Turn the page for the answer!

73

ANSWER: **B** ## frogs

A tadpole is the young of a frog. Unlike a frog, a tadpole has a tail and does not have legs. As it develops into a frog, it loses its tail and grows legs. During this stage, it looks like a fish with legs!

Did You Know?
Tadpoles grow hind legs first, and front legs later.

What did the frog say to its growing tadpole?

Good *frog-ress!*

75

Why do frogs lay so many eggs at a time?

What did the frog egg say after it bumped into another egg?

Eggs-cuse me!

ANSWER:
To increase the chances of survival of their young.

After laying eggs, frogs do not stay around to protect them from getting eaten by other animals, such as fish. They simply lay many eggs at a time. That way, the chances of some of them surviving to become adults are higher.

Where does a tadpole live?

- **A** on land
- **B** in water
- **C** in trees
- **D** under the ground

Turn the page for the answer!

ANSWER: **B**

in water

Tadpoles live in water. Like fish, they have special body parts called gills for breathing.

Did You Know?
Most tadpoles are tiny, but the bullfrog tadpole can grow as big as a banana!

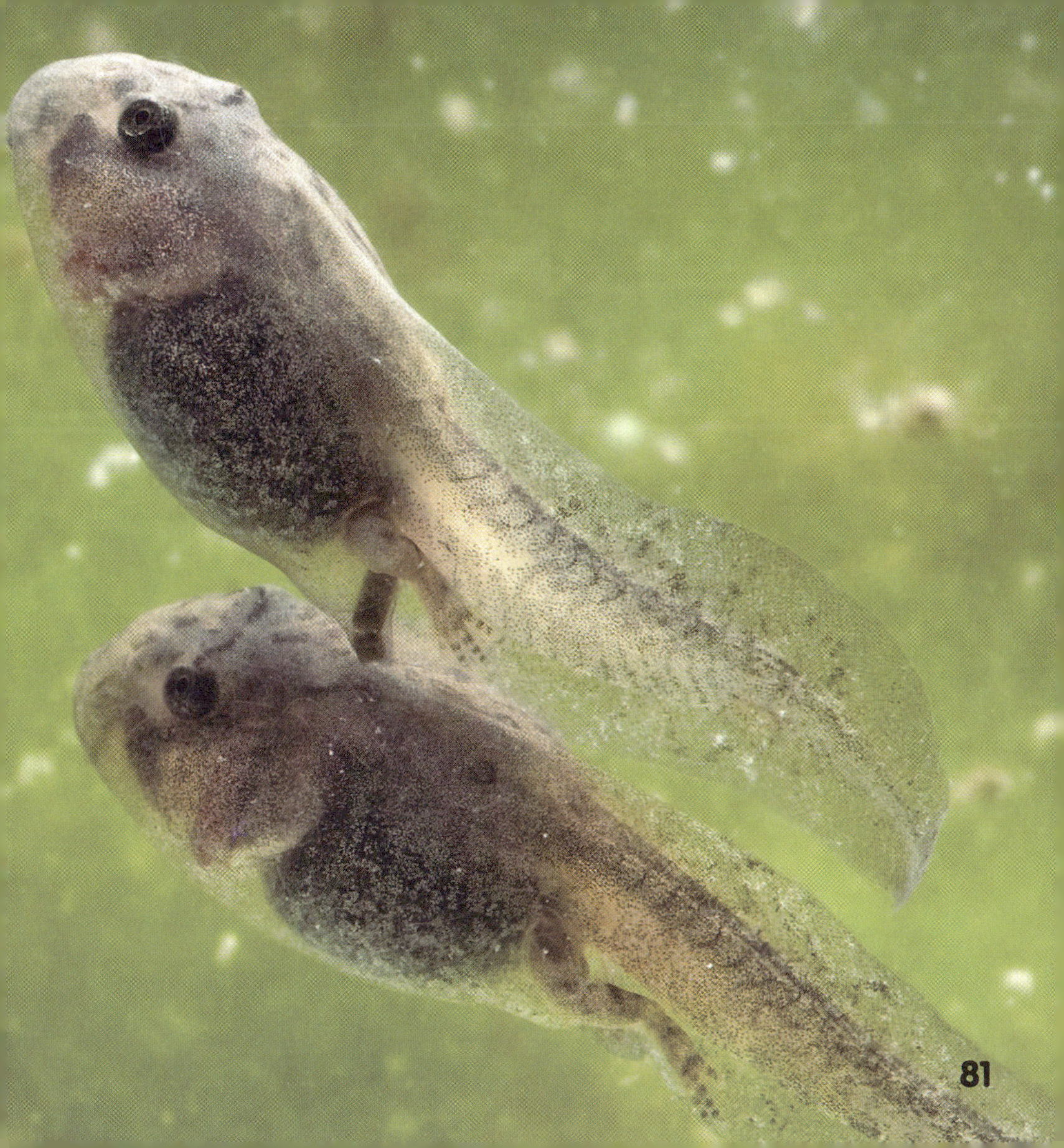

What body part does a tadpole have, but not a frog?

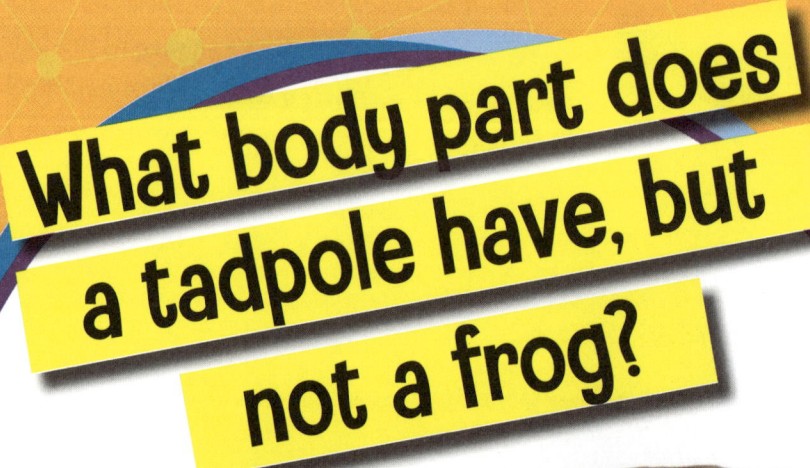

tadpole

82

ANSWER: A tail. A tadpole has a tail, but a frog does not. As a tadpole develops into a frog, its tail shrinks and gets absorbed into its body!

frog

Why aren't frogs good storytellers?

Because they don't have any *tales*!

83

Why do frog eggs have a jelly-like covering?

ANSWER: To protect the eggs.

The jelly-like covering holds the eggs together and protects them from being eaten by other animals.

Did You Know?

A frog can lay thousands of eggs at a time!

How did the frog feel when all its eggs hatched?

Eggs-static!

85

Which of these stages in the life cycle of a frog can be found in water?

eggs

tadpole

adult

Turn the page for the answer!

87

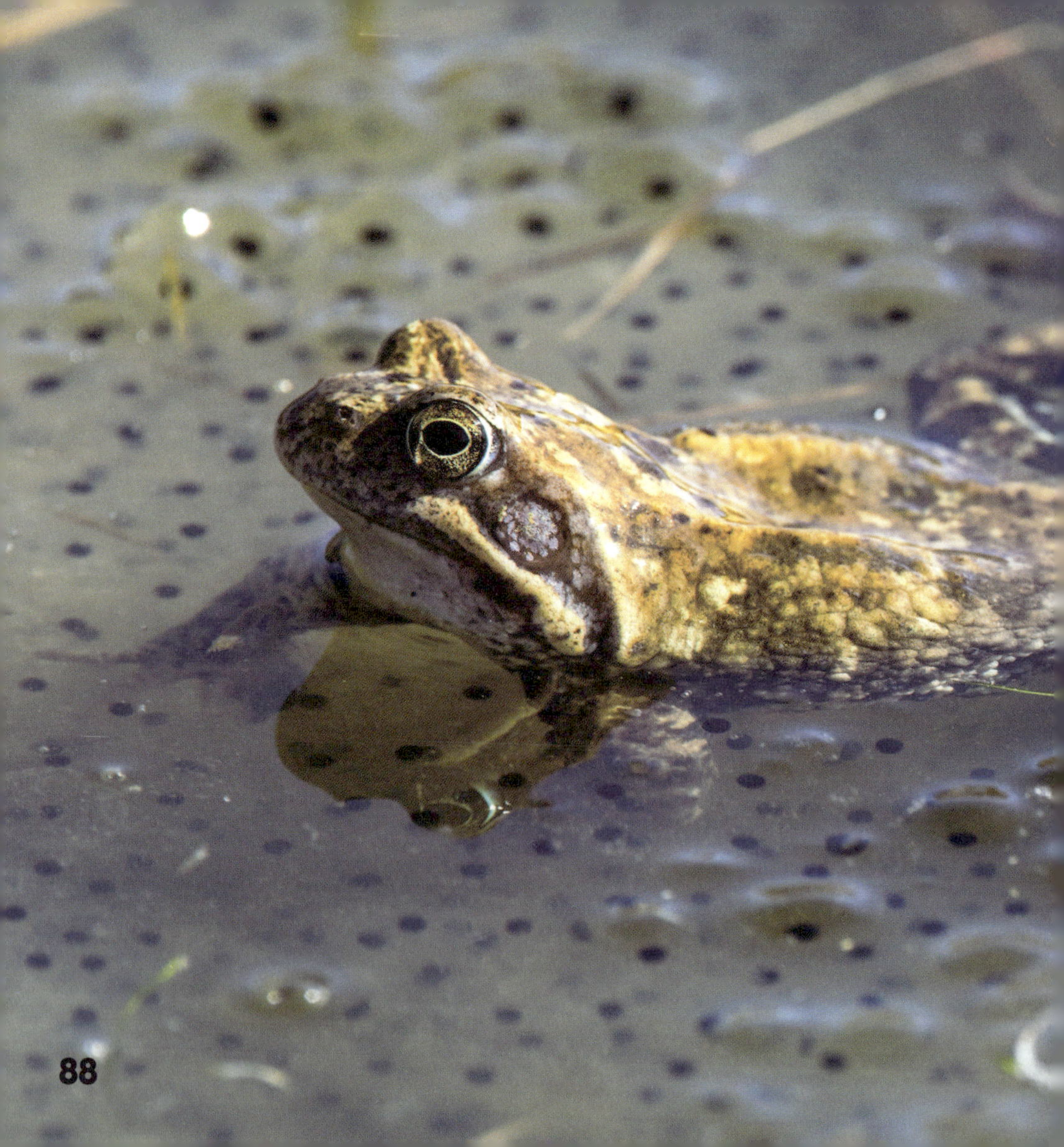

ANSWER:

All of them!

Most frogs lay eggs in water. The eggs hatch into tadpoles, which live in water. Adult frogs can live both on land and in water.

Where do frogs get glasses?

The *hop-tician!*

How many stages are there in the life cycle of a grasshopper?

- **A** one
- **B** two
- **C** three
- **D** four

Turn the page for the answer!

91

ANSWER: C

three

A grasshopper has three stages in its life cycle — egg, young and adult.

Did You Know?

Grasshoppers are considered a delicious snack in some countries!

What bus do tourist grasshoppers ride?

The *hop-on hop-off* bus!

93

What is the young of a grasshopper called?

- **A** the pupa
- **B** the larva
- **C** the nymph
- **D** the wriggler

Turn the page for the answer!

95

ANSWER: C

the nymph

The young of a grasshopper is called a nymph. Nymphs look similar to adult grasshoppers.

What do you call a grasshopper that likes to buy things?

A grass-shopper!

96

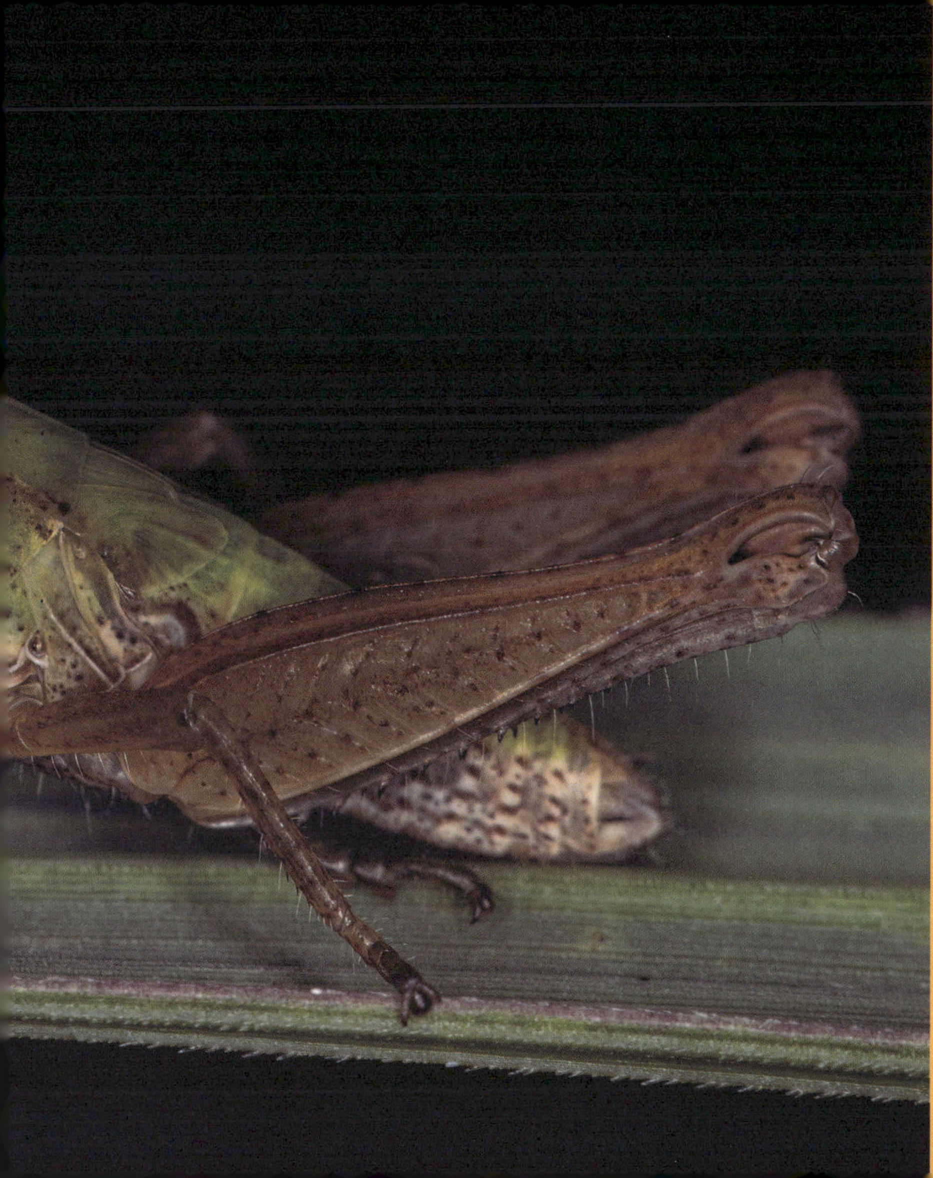

What is happening in this picture?

ANSWER: The insect is moulting.

Some animals shed their old outer covering and grow a new one. This process is known as moulting. Animals that moult include snakes, spiders, insects and crabs.

TRUE or FALSE?

A grasshopper has wings but its young does not.

Turn the page for the answer!

101

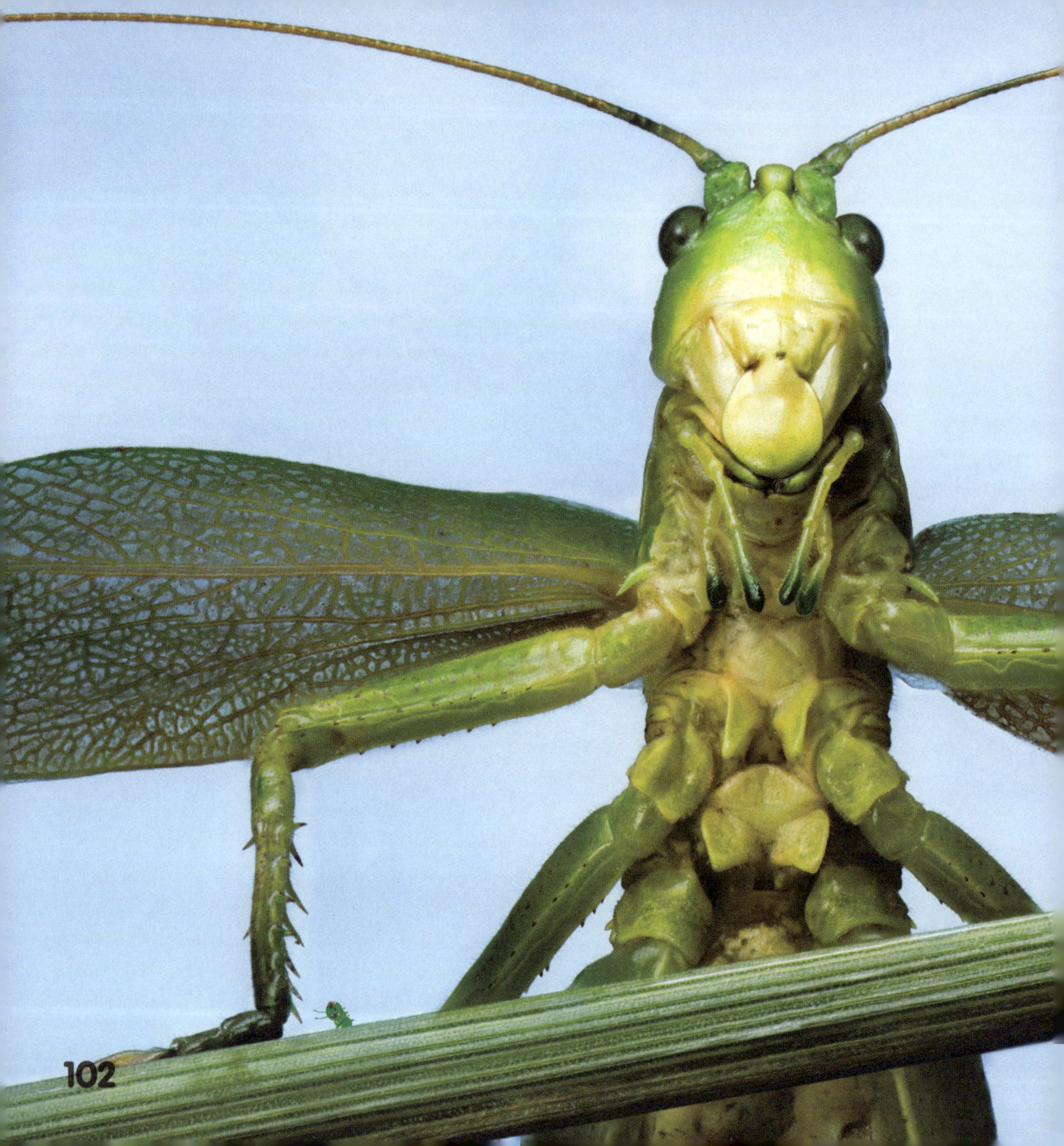

ANSWER:
True!

The young of a grasshopper, known as a nymph, does not have wings. Adult grasshoppers have wings and can fly.

Did You Know?

A nymph moults several times before it develops into an adult grasshopper.

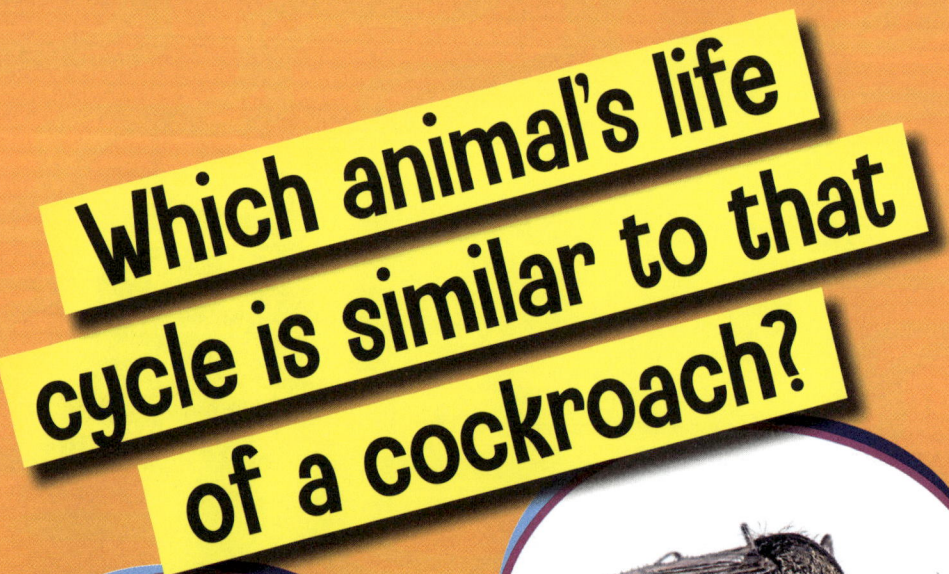

Which animal's life cycle is similar to that of a cockroach?

butterfly

mosquito

grasshopper

mealworm beetle

- **A** a butterfly's
- **B** a mosquito's
- **C** a grasshopper's
- **D** a mealworm beetle's

Turn the page for the answer!

ANSWER: C

a grasshopper's

Grasshoppers and cockroaches both have three stages in their life cycle — egg, young (nymph) and adult. The young of a grasshopper and a cockroach look like the adults.

egg

nymph

adult

What do you call a cockroach that is coming towards you?

An app-roach!

TRUE or FALSE?

This picture shows a cockroach with one egg.

ANSWER: False!

The picture shows a cockroach and an ootheca. An ootheca is an egg case that the female lays with the eggs inside it to protect them. The number of eggs inside each ootheca depends on the type of cockroach, but some oothecas can contain up to 50 eggs!

109

TRUE or FALSE?

Both a young cockroach and an adult cockroach can fly.

ANSWER: False! A young cockroach, known as a nymph, does not have wings and cannot fly. An adult cockroach has wings and can fly.

Did You Know?

Cockroaches are better runners than fliers. A cockroach can run at a speed of about 1.5 metres in one second!

111

Which stages in the life cycle of a ladybug beetle have been wrongly labelled?

adult

Did You Know?
Farmers love ladybugs! Ladybugs eat crop-destroying insects, such as aphids.

egg

pupa

larva

ANSWER: Larva and pupa.

The life cycle of a ladybug beetle has four stages — the egg, larva, pupa and adult. The egg hatches into the larva. The larva develops into the pupa, which develops into the adult.

113

TRUE or FALSE? Mealworms are a type of worm.

114

ANSWER: False!

The larvae that hatch out of the eggs of a mealworm beetle are commonly known as mealworms. However, they are not worms. The mealworm beetle is an insect.

Did You Know?

Mealworms are commonly used as food for pets such as turtles, lizards and frogs.

How many stages are in the life cycle of a butterfly?

Turn the page for the answer!

A one
B two
C three
D four

ANSWER: **D**

four

The life cycle of a butterfly has four stages — the egg, the larva, the pupa and the adult stage.

adult

pupa

118

egg

larva

119

TRUE or FALSE?

A caterpillar is a larva.

120

Turn the page for the answer!

ANSWER:

True!

The larva of a butterfly is also known as a caterpillar.

122

Did You Know?

Some caterpillars have fake eyes or 'eyespots' to make themselves look larger and more ferocious than they are. This helps keep predators away. Their actual eyes are much smaller than the eyespots.

TRUE or FALSE?

Caterpillars have more legs than butterflies.

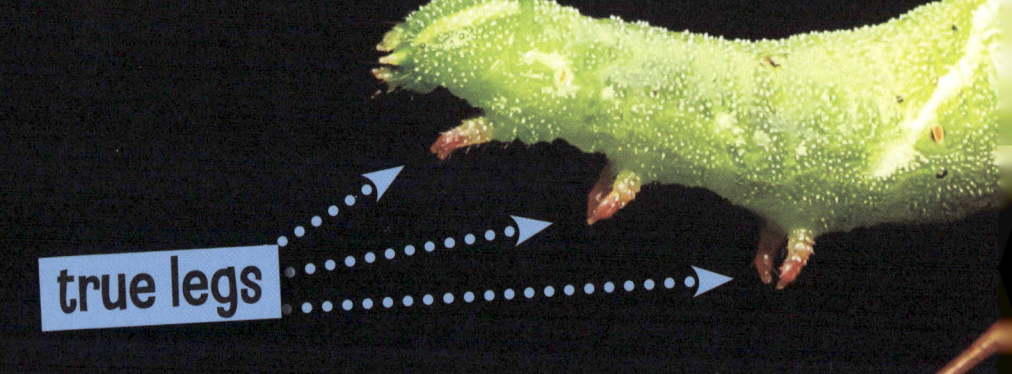

true legs

prolegs

ANSWER: True!

Caterpillars have three pairs of legs located just behind their heads. These are known as their true legs. Many caterpillars also have 'false legs,' known as prolegs, which help them to move and hold on to surfaces. The prolegs disappear when the pupa develops into a butterfly.

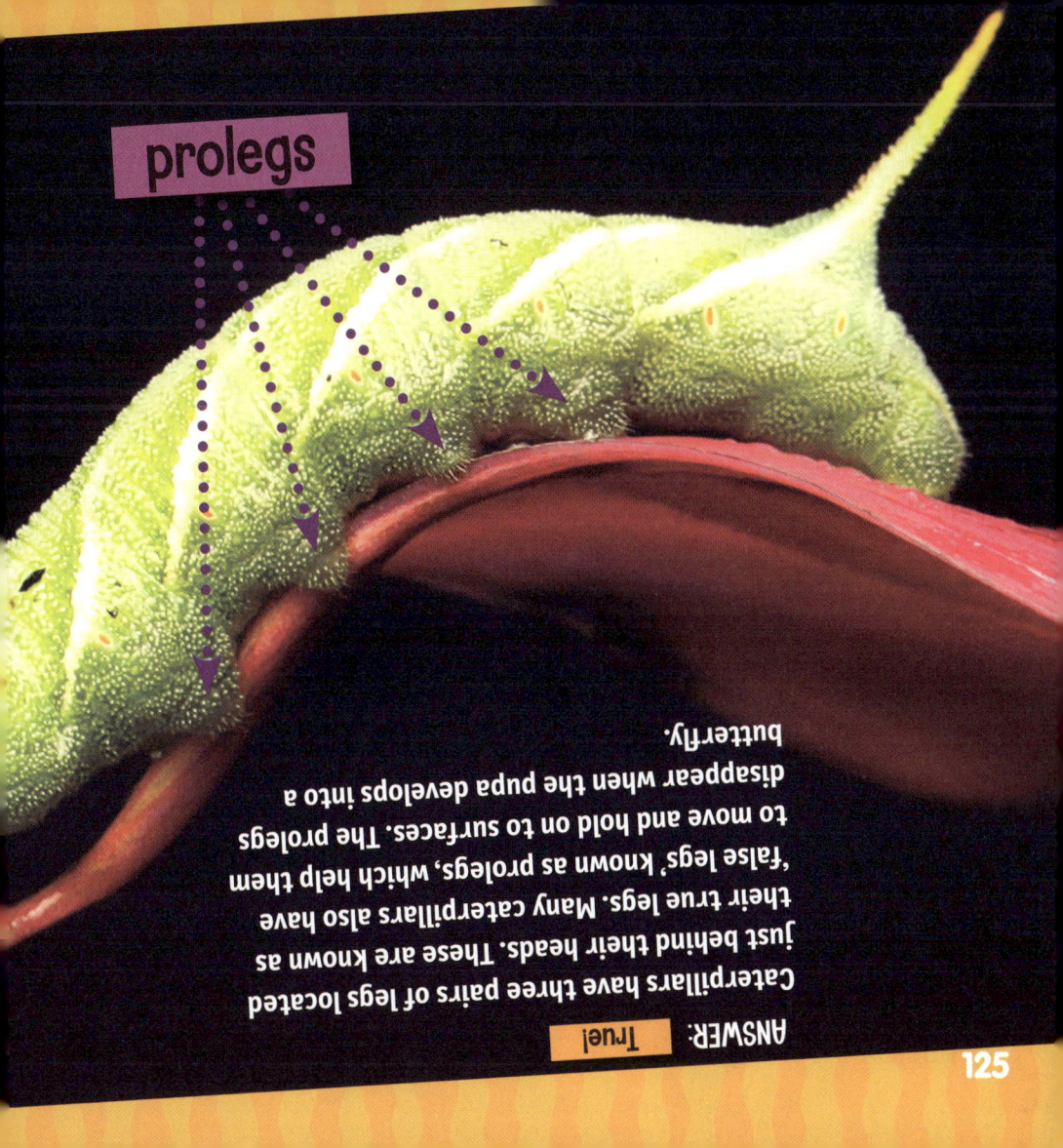

How long do most adult butterflies live?

- **A** a few days
- **B** a few weeks
- **C** a few months
- **D** a few years

Turn the page for the answer!

ANSWER: B

a few weeks

Most adult butterflies live only for a few weeks. Most of this time is spent looking for mates, mating, and in the case of the females, laying eggs.

Did You Know?

The lifespan of a butterfly depends on the type of butterfly. Some types of butterflies live only for a few days, while others, such as the Brimstone butterfly, can live for more than a year.

What are the plural forms of 'larva' and 'pupa'?

ANSWER: Larvae and pupae.

The plural form of 'larva' is 'larvae' and the plural form of 'pupa' is 'pupae'.

What did the butterfly say to its young?

I larva you!

Did You Know?

The pupa of a butterfly or a moth is also known as a chrysalis. During this stage, the insect stops eating completely and undergoes many changes to turn into a butterfly or a moth.

TRUE or FALSE?

A caterpillar can double its body size in a single day.

132

Turn the page for the answer!

133

ANSWER:
True!

As soon as they hatch out of the eggs, caterpillars eat continuously. Some caterpillars can eat so much that they double their body size in a day!

Did You Know?

The first thing that the caterpillars eat when they hatch out of the eggs are their eggshells!

135

TRUE or FALSE?

A butterfly will lay its eggs on any plant.

How do butterflies decorate their homes?

With larva lamps!

**ANSWER:
False!**

Butterflies are extremely picky when it comes to laying their eggs. They lay them only on specific types of plants. This is to make sure that their larvae have an immediate supply of food as soon as they hatch.

137

Why do butterflies lay eggs on the underside of leaves?

ANSWER:
To hide them!

Butterflies often lay their eggs on the underside of leaves. This helps to hide the eggs from animals that may eat them.

Did You Know?
Butterflies attach their eggs to plants using a special glue. The superstrong glue helps the eggs to stay on the plant and not fall off easily.

139

Which animal do these eggs belong to?

- **A** a frog
- **B** a chicken
- **C** a butterfly
- **D** a mosquito

ANSWER: ⓓ a mosquito

A female mosquito lays her eggs on still, or stagnant, water. The eggs are laid one at a time and stuck together in the shape of a raft. Each egg raft can contain 100–400 eggs! Not all the eggs will grow into adults though, as some of the larvae and pupae may be eaten up by predators.

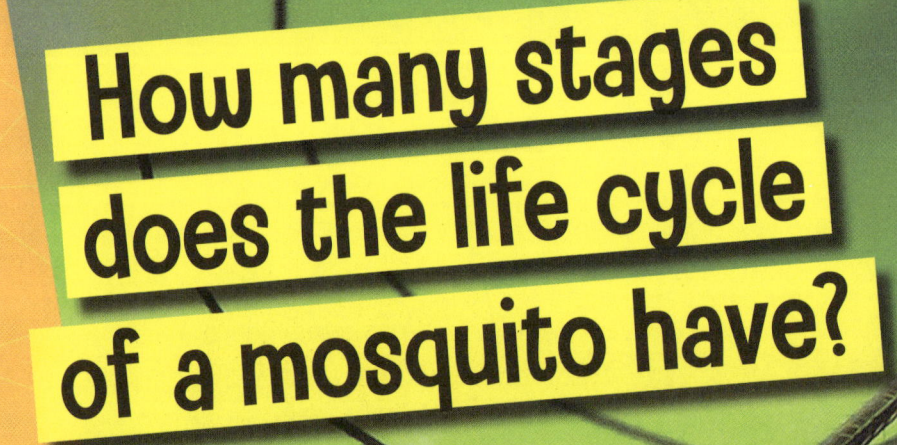

How many stages does the life cycle of a mosquito have?

- **A** one
- **B** two
- **C** three
- **D** four

Turn the page for the answer!

143

adult

ANSWER: **D**
four

pupa

144

egg

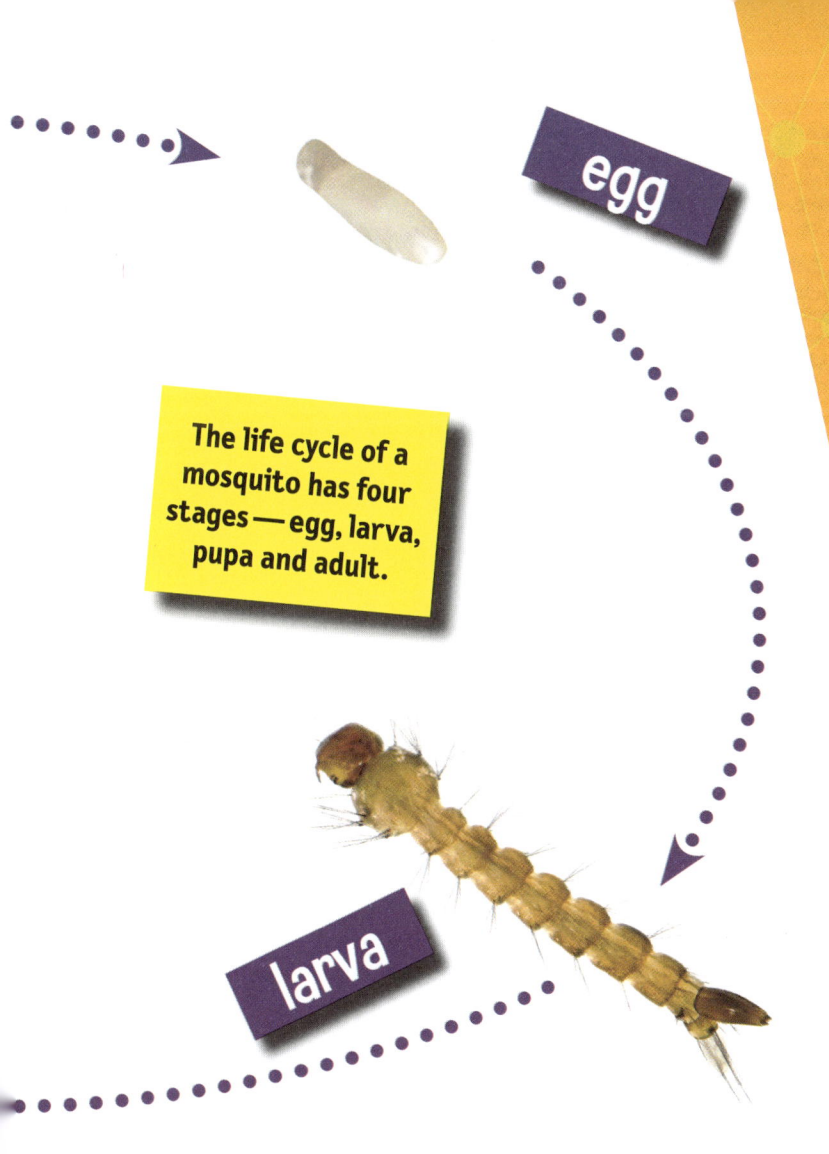

The life cycle of a mosquito has four stages — egg, larva, pupa and adult.

larva

What is the larva of a mosquito also known as?

146

- **A** a pupa
- **B** a nymph
- **C** a tadpole
- **D** a wriggler

ANSWER:
D a wriggler
The egg of a mosquito hatches into a larva, also known as a wriggler.

DID YOU KNOW?

The mosquito larva lives near the water's surface and breathes in air using a breathing tube!

147

148

Which of these does a mosquito pupa NOT do?

- **A** eat
- **B** move
- **C** breathe
- **D** develop

ANSWER: **A** eat

At the pupa stage, a mosquito does not eat. It lives near the water's surface, breathing using two breathing tubes. It can move rapidly if it detects danger. It continues to develop into an adult mosquito.

TRUE or FALSE?

All mosquitoes bite.

Turn the page for the answer!

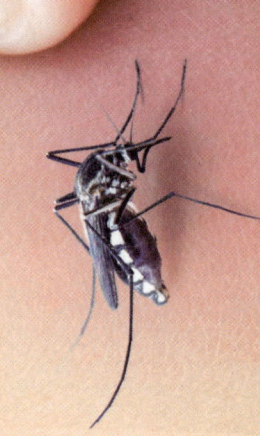

150

How do mosquitoes go to school?

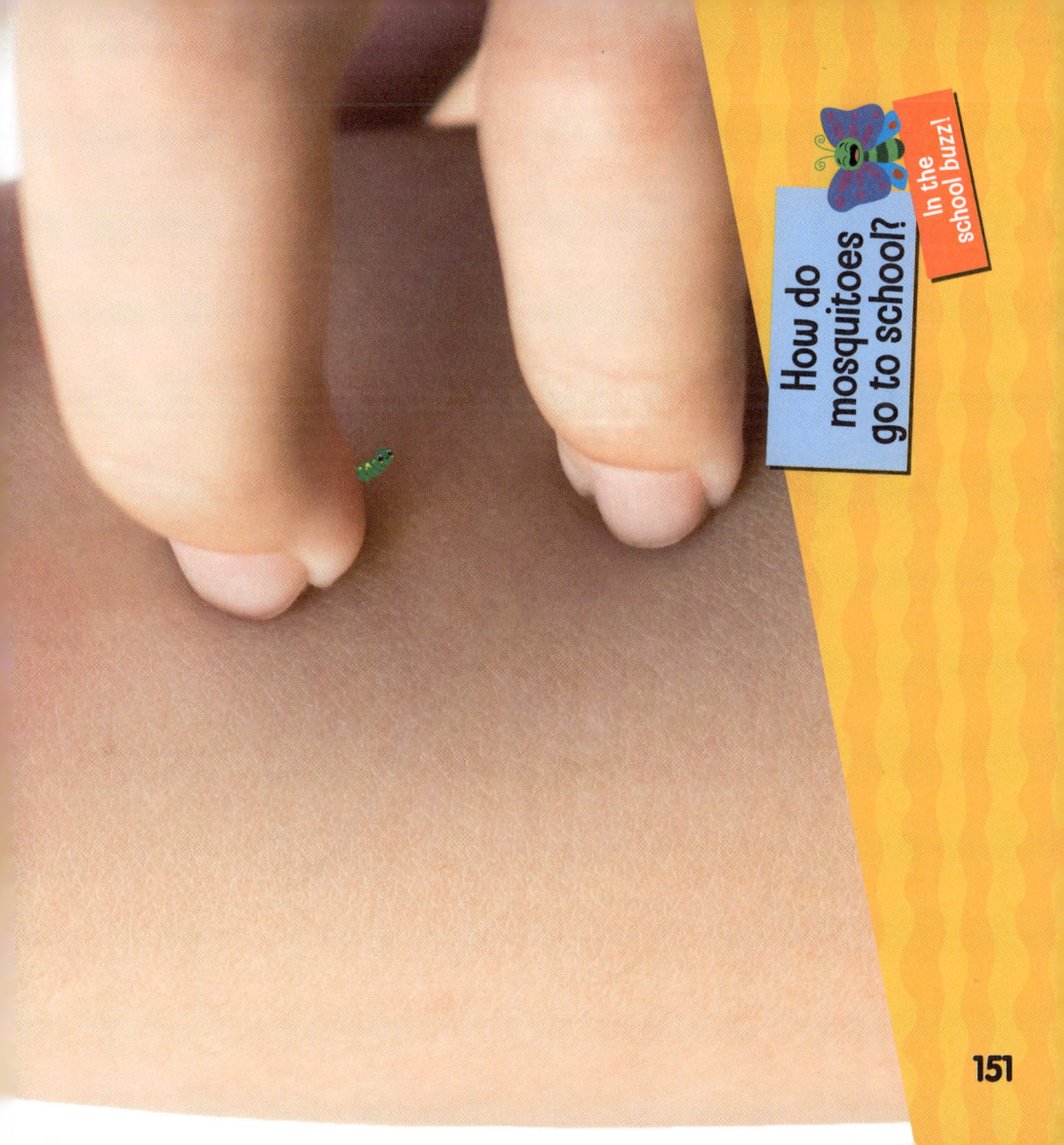

In the school buzz!

151

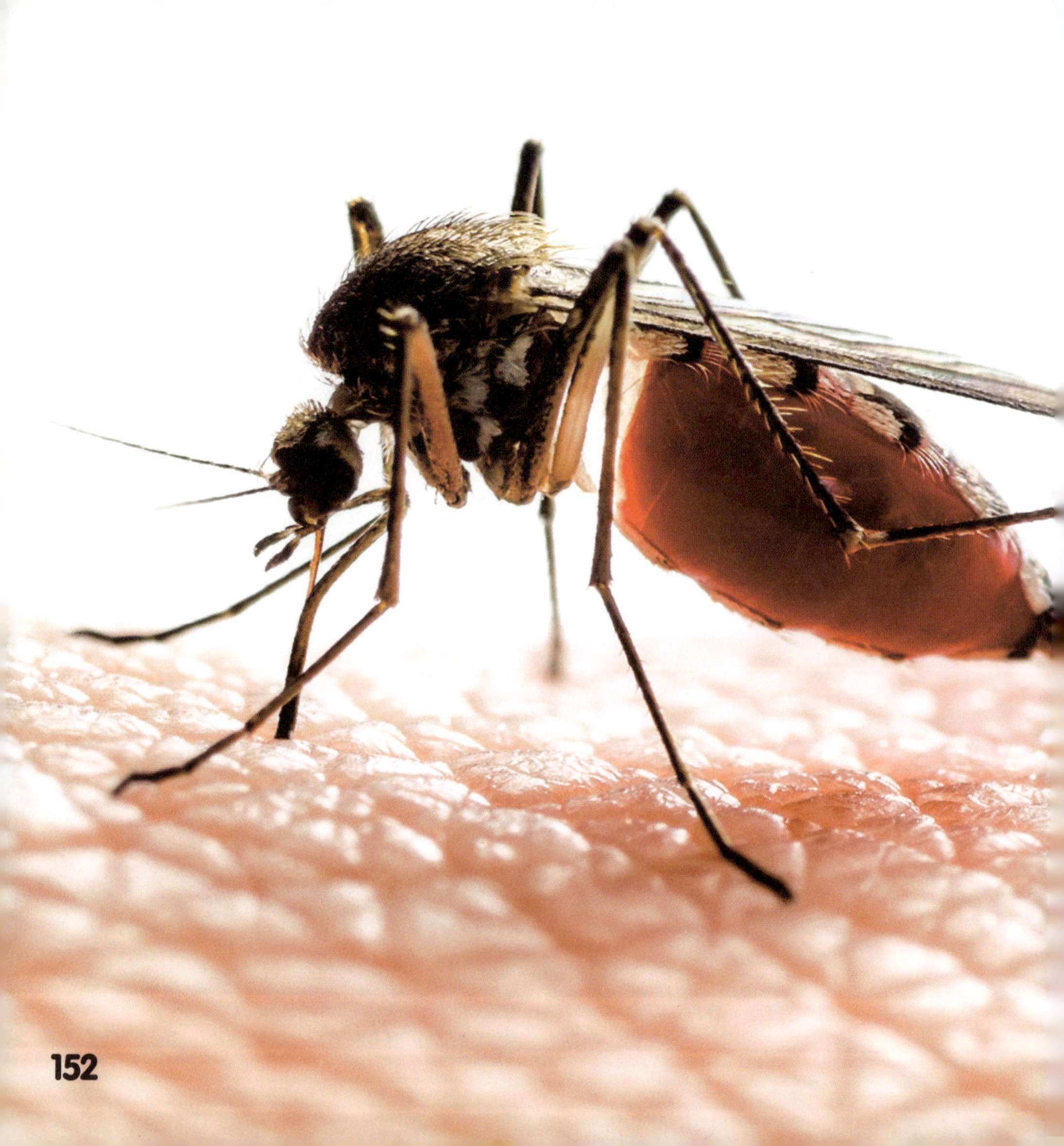

ANSWER:

False!

Only female mosquitoes bite people and other animals to feed on blood. This is because they need the iron in blood to develop their eggs.

DID YOU KNOW?

Male mosquitoes feed on plant juices.

TRUE or FALSE?

Why do mosquitoes fly towards people?

To grab a bite!

154

Dengue is a disease spread by mosquitoes.

ANSWER: True!

Dengue is a disease that is spread when female *Aedes aegypti* mosquitoes infected by the dengue virus bite us.

DID YOU KNOW?

In some countries, to control the spread of dengue, male *Aedes aegypti* mosquitoes infected with the Wolbachia bacteria are released in large numbers. When these mosquitoes mate with the female mosquitoes, their eggs do not hatch. This helps prevent the mosquitoes from breeding and spreading diseases.

How can stagnant water lead to the spread of dengue?

ANSWER: It's where mosquitoes lay their eggs.

Mosquitoes lay their eggs in stagnant water. Stagnant water collected in old tyres, flowerpot plates and containers can lead to more mosquitoes breeding and spreading diseases such as dengue.

Which of these are ways to prevent mosquitoes from spreading diseases?

Use mosquito repellent.

Remove stagnant water.

Use larvicides to kill mosquito larva.

Spread oil on the surface of stagnant water.

ANSWER: All of them!

Mosquito repellent can help keep mosquitoes from biting us and spreading diseases. Removing stagnant water, using larvicides (chemicals that kill larvae) and spreading oil on the surface of stagnant water can help prevent mosquitoes from breeding.

TRUE or FALSE?

Ancient scientists used to believe that insects were produced by mud.

Maria Sibylla Merian

ANSWER: True!

Scientists used to believe that insects came from non-living matter, such as mud, until the work of German naturalist Maria Sibylla Merian became known. Her detailed studies and drawings of the life cycles of insects in the late 1600s and early 1700s disproved the old beliefs.

Which animal do these eggs belong to?

- **A** a housefly
- **B** a butterfly
- **C** a mosquito
- **D** a honeybee

ANSWER: ⓓ a honeybee

A queen bee lays thousands of eggs each day, one in each cell of the honeycomb.

What does the queen bee call her young?

Bay-bees!

163

Which stage is NOT in a honeybee's life cycle?

- **A** the egg stage
- **B** the pupa stage
- **C** the larva stage
- **D** the nymph stage

ANSWER: ⓓ the nymph stage

The life cycle of a honeybee has four stages — egg, larva, pupa and adult. The nymph stage is usually found in insect life cycles that have three stages.

What do bees do when they are excited?

They hive-five one another!

165

Bonus Quiz Time!

Match the keywords to their definitions.

___ Caterpillar
___ Germination
___ Larva
___ Life cycle
___ Moulting
___ Nymph
___ Pupa
___ Seed
___ Tadpole
___ Wriggler

1. The process by which a seed or a spore develops into a young plant
2. A cycle made up of the different stages in the life of a living thing
3. The young of a cockroach or a grasshopper
4. The stage in the life cycle of an insect where it stops feeding and starts developing into an adult
5. The young of a butterfly
6. A structure by which a flowering plant reproduces
7. The process of shedding the old outer covering and growing a new one
8. The young of an insect that hatches out of an egg
9. The larva of a mosquito
10. The young of a frog

Answers

BONUS QUIZ TIME ANSWERS: Caterpillar – 5; Germination – 1; Larva – 8; Life cycle – 2; Moulting – 7; Nymph – 3; Pupa – 4; Seed – 6; Tadpole – 10; Wriggler – 9.

Which pages was Carter Caterpillar hiding on?

Pages 13, 15, 19, 27, 37, 40, 44, 53, 69, 71, 75, 76, 85, 95, 98, 100, 102, 114, 122, 130, 132, 136, 151, 163 and 165.

Finished reading the book?

Follow these steps to get your own *Quiz Champs* certificate!

1. Solve the crossword puzzle using the given clues.
2. Identify the letters on the boxes with Carter Caterpillar ( ).
3. Unscramble the letters to form a word. That's your password!
4. Enter the password in the PDF file on www.tinyurl.com/quizchampscert to download your *Quiz Champs* certificate!

168

ACROSS

5. The young of a kangaroo
7. An animal that is 900 times bigger than its baby
9. The young of a butterfly
10. A bird that lays its eggs in other birds' nests

DOWN

1. The yellow part of an egg
2. The young of a grasshopper
3. A device that is used to hatch eggs without a hen
4. A winged insect with a four-stage life cycle
6. The animal that lays the world's largest eggs
8. A disease spread by infected mosquitoes

I have identified the letters: __ __ __ __ __ __ __

I have unscrambled them to form my password! __ __ __ __ __ __ __

Quiz Champs

The *Quiz Champs* series has been specially crafted to be a fun and educational learning experience for young learners. The series is aligned with the Singapore primary Science syllabus and the Cambridge primary Science curriculum, and also includes enrichment questions to stretch curious minds. Answers and additional information have been provided to aid in learning, revision and preparation for testing.

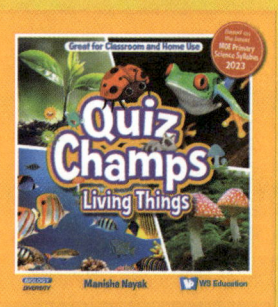

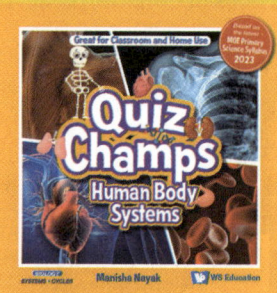

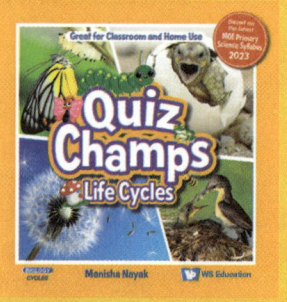

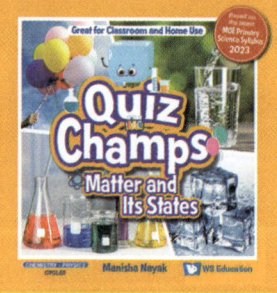

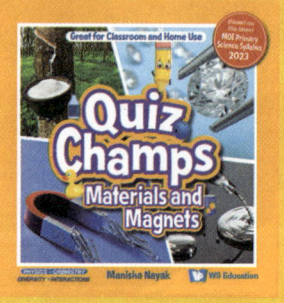

- Quiz Champs: Living Things — Manisha Nayak, WS Education
- Quiz Champs: Human Body Systems — Manisha Nayak, WS Education
- Quiz Champs: Life Cycles — Manisha Nayak, WS Education
- Quiz Champs: Matter and Its States — Manisha Nayak, WS Education
- Quiz Champs: Materials and Magnets — Manisha Nayak, WS Education

I'M A FUTURE SCIENTIST!

The *I'm a Future Scientist!* series is based on the Science Centre Singapore's longstanding and highly popular Young Scientist badge programme. This exciting series of full-colour books for 6–12-year-olds will spark sustained interest in scientific fields, such as botany, zoology, marine biology, conservation and the environment, astronomy, and many more, while delivering primary-school-level Science learning points in an engaging and relatable way!

Through clearly written educational articles, fun cartoons, suggested hands-on activities, as well as full-colour photographs and illustrations, these books are the perfect companions for budding scientists to delve further into a wide range of fields of Science.

In addition, Augmented Reality (AR) elements will also help to bring Science alive for children, helping them to retain the information provided better, and inspiring better learning! And, as a bonus, earn points for the Young Scientist Badge programme from Science Centre Singapore, using the links inside!

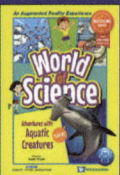

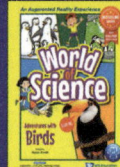

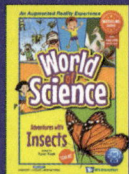

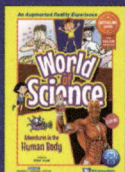

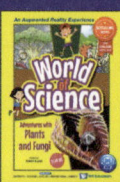

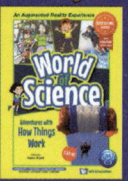

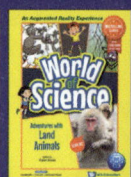

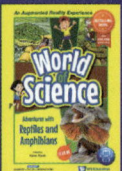

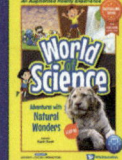

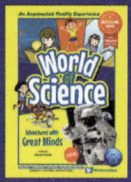

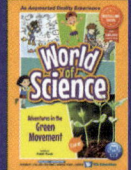

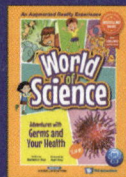

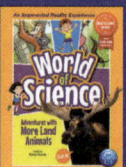

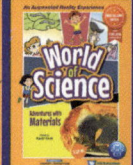

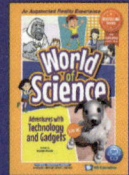

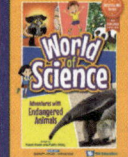

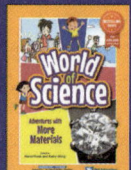

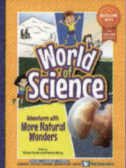

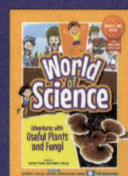

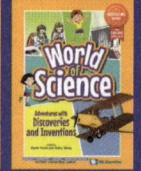

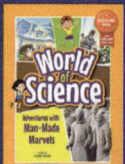

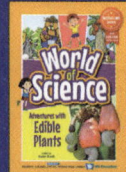

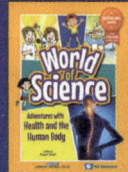

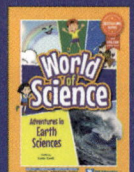

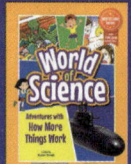